Positive Thinking

Acquire Mastery Over Your Mind: Demonstrated
Techniques To Foster Happiness, Self-Assurance, And
Serenity, Manage Your Thoughts And Unlock Your
Genuine Capacity For Happiness And Achievement

Willibald Rieger

TABLE OF CONTENT

The Time-Tested Methods Of Cognitive Behavioral Therapy 1

Using The Language Of Success To Harness The Power Of Affirmations 12

Techniques For Positive Thought That Are Fun And Relaxing 37

Accepting The Variations 57

How To Disengage Yourself From Negative Thoughts Mentally 70

Techniques For Happiness 82

Effectively Combating Negative Ideas 101

The Time-Tested Methods Of Cognitive Behavioral Therapy

As we've discussed, Cognitive Behavioral Therapy has various forms and sizes because it covers multiple techniques. This implies that you have options, so you may take your time and find the solution that best meets your unique requirements.

You and your therapist work together throughout this therapy, so you may sit down and decide which approaches to use. What truly works for you and what you hope to accomplish should inform your choice. Combining some of these methods will result in an efficient strategy. After you've learned about these methods, you can use them to make beneficial changes in your daily life. Knowing these tactics is helpful because you can discuss the ones you are interested in with your therapist, and they can advise you on which one is best for you and how effective it is at dealing with your particular problem.

Conducting behavioral studies

Cognitive behavioral therapy tests ideas through behavioral trials. You may, for instance, conduct a behavioral experiment to see how you can utilize your thoughts to stop overeating and consequent weight gain. In this instance, one could argue, "I'll find that when I punish myself for overindulging, I eat less than when I'm easy on myself." To reach this conclusion, you must independently test both strategies and observe the results. For instance, you could feel guilty about overindulging and then track the impact on your eating habits. You might try having a nice conversation with yourself after overindulging another time. You are welcome to participate in this behavioral experiment. Behavioral experiments alter your beliefs based on your intuition or emotional response to something, even without supporting data.

Records of thoughts

Records are similar to behavioral experiments in that they are also meant to evaluate the validity of your ideas. As a clinical psychology student, imagine your supervisor giving you unfavorable criticism. It's simple to assume that your boss believes you're worthless. One option is to conduct a thought record, in which you assess your evidence for this thought and the evidence refuting it. You can think back to a recent favorable comment from the same supervisor if you seek evidence opposing this idea. You might also say that your supervisor trusts you to conduct evaluations and give clients feedback. They wouldn't entrust you with that duty if they believed you were incompetent.

You could also try to find proof to support your claims that your supervisor believes you are worthless. After weighing the information on all sides, you must formulate more thoughtful arguments. You may persuade yourself, for instance, "I just made a mistake when I (whatever you did), but mistakes are common." What I can do is learn from that error and use my supervisor's criticism; they will be impressed by the improvement. You can rationally alter your beliefs by using thought words.

arranging enjoyable activities

This is a Cognitive Behavioural Therapy approach that is particularly helpful in treating depression. You must write down the dates of the next seven days, starting with the current week's Wednesday, Thursday, Friday, and so forth. For this, you can use a notebook or a piece of paper. From there, you can place one enjoyable activity daily on a plan you draw out for these seven days. Not only should these be enjoyable pursuits for you, but they should also be healthful. If they are activities you don't get to perform daily, they also become enjoyable. It's best not to overcomplicate this process by thinking of something difficult because it can be as easy as eating lunch or finishing a book you've meant to read for a while.

Alternatively, you can engage in pursuits that give you a feeling of mastery and achievement. The secret is to continue aiming for something modest that you wouldn't typically do. It's ideal to have an activity that takes less than ten minutes. You can undertake three enjoyable daily tasks once you have learned this approach and want to enhance it. You will think less negatively if you regularly partake in activities that make you feel many good emotions.

Hierarchies of situation exposure

This primarily entails adding items to your list that you often avoid completing. Enumerate the things off-limits, beginning with ice cream and concluding with full-fat yogurt. If you have social anxiety, you may start your list by meeting new people and finish it by asking a person who is not your gender for directions.

From there, you can begin assigning a number on a scale of 0 to 10 to each thing on your list, according to how distressed you would be if you had to complete those activities. If you were to consume ice cream, your level of distress would increase to a 10. In that case, you may write, ice cream = 10. Once you've ranked the various foods or chores you'd rather not do, you can sort them from highest to lowest score. The primary goal of this is to assist you in recognizing your issue. Rather than having several products with the same rating, each item should have its own number. This will provide you with a hierarchy to work with while solving these issues, and it's a good idea to work from the lowest to the highest. Before going on to the next item on the list, it is a good idea to test one out a few times (or even for a few days). You can move on to the next item on your list when you are making progress and are only experiencing half the amount of distress you used to when executing a given task.

exposure based on imagery

Everybody has memories they would rather forget. Nonetheless, you use the imagery-based exposure strategy when you revisit this experience, particularly if it often elicits very strong negative feelings. We can still refer back to our previous scenario, in which a student in clinical psychology received unfavorable criticism from his supervisor. To utilize imagery exposure, the learner must recall the specifics of the severe feedback experience, including all of the senses. He can remember the tone of the supervisor when providing him with comments, the appearance of the room, the supervisor's angry gaze, and other details.

Furthermore, he would endeavor to recognize and label his various ideas and feelings during this interaction. He can elaborate and discuss his behavioral impulses. He may, for instance, have had the impulse to lash out, storm out of the room, or cry. If exposed to prolonged imagery exposure, the learner may visualize every element of the image for an extended period until he notices that thinking about it no longer causes him as much discomfort as it once did. He may now rank his level of distress from the visual as low as 4/10, compared to his initial 8/10 rating.

This method lessens the pain associated with intrusive memories, which lessens the likelihood that they would cause rumination. Consequently, it also lessens the likelihood of avoidance coping. You'll understand that you are more likely to choose healthy coping mechanisms when memory isn't as upsetting as it once was.

It is especially recommended that those who are depressed undertake Cognitive Behavioural Therapy to assist in shifting their negative thought patterns to positive ones. Depressive thoughts exacerbate existing depression. Contrary to popular assumption, everyone experiences happy emotions, even those who are depressed. What makes us different is how we choose to respond to those feelings. Even when they are experiencing happy feelings, depressed people typically try to suppress them. Researchers made this discovery, which caught many off guard. "Dampening" refers to the cognitive method of repressing certain feelings. People typically utilize other thoughts to suppress those emotions; examples are, "This good feeling is only temporary," "I don't deserve this happiness," and so forth. Let's use the case of a recently arrived mother who is experiencing postpartum depression. She may convince herself that she is a bad mother and doesn't deserve to get better just because she is depressed. This mother's recovery may be severely hampered by this train of thought. She may, however, change these beliefs and feelings through cognitive behavioral therapy, which will be the first step toward her rehabilitation.

One may question why these kinds of thoughts occur to depressed individuals. Their internalized critical voice keeps them from being let down after raising their expectations too high. It so turns into a form of defensive pessimism.

You and your therapist will need to meet when you first begin Cognitive Behavioural Therapy to discuss the patterns of behavior you need to break. Since they will assist you in this process, tactics and approaches will be discussed at this point. Helping you control the area of your brain that is in charge of pleasant thoughts is the main objective of the therapy. Together with the assigned homework, your therapist's frequent appointments might help you maintain your new, healthy routines. When you put what you've learned in treatment into practice, you also make a significant contribution.

These methods are especially crucial if you are attempting to overcome depression using Cognitive Behavioural Therapy.

Using The Language Of Success To Harness The Power Of Affirmations

Strong, uplifting phrases known as affirmations can assist you in overcoming limiting beliefs, negative thoughts, and self-doubt. You may rewire your brain and create the conditions for personal development and achievement by speaking about success. This chapter will cover the significance of affirmations and offer helpful hints on formulating and employing them.

Comprehending Affirmations: Affirmations are succinct, uplifting words centered around a certain objective or intended result. Repeating these statements may teach your mind to believe in your skills and strengthen a positive self-image. This, in turn, might assist you in overcoming challenges and realizing your objectives.

The Advantages of Affirmations: Regular use of affirmations can result in various advantages, including improved motivation, lower stress levels, and elevated self-esteem. You'll probably notice a change in your thinking as you repeat affirmations; this can help you draw more happiness and success into your life.

Crafting Powerful Affirmations:

Employ optimistic language and the present tense in your affirmations.

Do not use terms like "not" or "can't," as these might perpetuate negative mental habits.

Alternatively, focus on your goals and see yourself as having already attained the desired result.

Customizing Your Affirmations: Adapt your affirmations to your objectives and preferences to get the most out of them. Make affirmations that specifically address the aspects of your life you would like to improve or the obstacles you would like to overcome.

Using Affirmations:

Establish a regular practice to reap the greatest benefits from your affirmations.

Whether in the morning, right before bed, or at peaceful periods during the day, repeat your affirmations.

As you repeat them, try to experience the feelings accompanying the affirmations and picture the intended result.

Combining Visualisation with Affirmations: Use visualization techniques in conjunction with your affirmations to achieve even more powerful results. As you recite your affirmations, picture yourself accomplishing your objectives and feeling all the good that success brings. This can support the effectiveness of your affirmations and make you feel more confident in your skills.

Monitoring Your Progress: Maintain a notebook in which you can note your accomplishments and consider your experiences to assess the impact of your affirmations. This might assist you in determining areas in which you might need to modify your affirmations or develop new ones to better fit your changing objectives and desires.

You may rewire your mind for optimism, eliminate limiting ideas, and create the conditions for personal development and achievement by using the power of affirmations and the language of success. Recall that creating a successful affirmations practice requires patience and persistence, just like any other habit, but the benefits can change your life.

Day 5: Visualisation and daily confirmations

Greetings on Day 5 of the 14-day course on optimistic thinking!

We'll go more into the daily affirmation and visualization practice today. Strong declarations, known as affirmations, can change our attitudes and beliefs. They form a powerful instrument for positive thinking and creating good things when paired with visualization.

Examine the list of affirmations you made on Day 2 to get started. Pick three affirmations that speak to you right now. Put them in writing and give them purpose and conviction. Your aims, goals, and the good traits you want to live up to should all be reflected in your affirmations.

Now that you have affirmations, it's time to include visualization exercises. The process of forming an internal picture of your intended results is known as visualization. It entails using your emotions and senses to create a vivid and realistic mental image.

Locate a calm, cozy area where you may unwind and concentrate. Shut your eyes and inhale deeply many times. Start by saying your affirmations aloud or silently. As soon as you have a sense of equilibrium, imagine yourself leading a life that brings you the satisfaction you seek. Imagine yourself reaching your objectives, being happy, and being the person your affirmations describe.

Use every sensation as you visualize. Picture the sights, sounds, and aromas of the world you want to live in. Experience the joy of reaching your objectives and leading the best possible life. Permit yourself to go completely into the experience, accepting any feelings and sensations that surface.

Take a few minutes to practice this visualization technique every day. You can decide whether to do it in the evening to reaffirm your good intentions before bed or in the morning to start your day off on a great note. Keeping up this practice is important since it allows you to synchronize your thoughts, feelings, and behaviors with the desired beneficial results.

Keep your affirmations close to your heart throughout the day. Whenever you face difficulties or unfavorable ideas, mentally repeat these statements aloud. Allow them to act as an anchor to help you return to a positive frame of mind and as a reminder of your good intentions.

Create visual cues as well to help you remember your affirmations. Put them someplace you'll see them often, like the fridge, computer screen, or bathroom mirror, by writing them on sticky notes. Another option is to make a vision board using pictures of the results you hope to achieve. Make sure you have inspirational and motivating visual reminders all around you.

As Day 5 draws close, consider the effectiveness of your daily affirmations and visualizations. Recognize their influence on your outlook and capacity to attract favorable consequences. We'll talk about self-care tomorrow and how it helps you keep a good outlook. Cultivate your visualization and affirmation practice, and allow optimism to lead the way.

Day 6: MIND-SETTING AND SELF-CARE

Greetings on Day 6 of the 14-day course on optimistic thinking!

We're going to talk about self-care and mindfulness today. Keeping ourselves well is essential to having a good outlook and well-being.

Think back to the pursuits and routines that make you happy and refreshed. Make a list of the self-care practices that speak to you. Simple activities like walking outdoors, reading a book, doing yoga, or spending time with close friends and family might serve as these. Remember that every person's needs for self-care are different, so pick things that nourish and inspire you.

After making your list, include at least one self-care task in your everyday schedule. Self-care doesn't have to take much time; a few minutes a day can have a big impact. Set yourself first and make time in your calendar for these healthy pursuits.

Besides engaging in self-care, mindfulness training is an effective means of developing an optimistic outlook. It eases mental tension, lowers anxiety, and improves your capacity to react calmly and optimistically to circumstances.

Take time to focus on being aware. Choose a comfortable location, get into a comfortable position, and focus on breathing. Take note of how the air feels inside and out of your body. When your thoughts stray, gently bring them back to the here and now, along with the feeling of your breath. Let ideas come and go without becoming sucked into them.

Focus on the subject as you do your regular tasks to cultivate mindfulness. Whether dining, strolling, or conversing, give it your all. Take in the moments of happiness, relish the experiences, and pay attention to the nuances.

Consistency and intention are necessary when integrating self-care and mindfulness into your everyday routine. Think briefly about including mindfulness and self-care in your daily routine. Determine any obstacles or difficulties that might occur and come up with solutions. Recall that self-care and mindfulness are worthwhile priorities to invest in your well-being.

As Day 6 ends, acknowledge and appreciate your decision to look after yourself and cultivate a happy outlook. Accept self-care and mindfulness as methods for building resilience, lowering stress levels, and promoting happiness. We'll discuss the influence of good self-talk on our thinking tomorrow. Continue to practice mindfulness and self-care, and allow them to lead you to a happier and more contented existence.

How Your Brain Can Be Retrained

Here's how to force your mind to focus on the positives and retrain it:

1: Pay Attention to Your Thoughts

You will never make any changes if you are unaware of what you are thinking about and do not recognize whether it is healthy. As was previously indicated, the average person has between 50,000 and 70,000 thoughts per day, and most of us are not aware of our ideas until they cause us to feel angry, afraid, or anxious.

To be conscious of your thoughts is to become aware of what is going through your head. You can comb through it in this manner. This does not imply that you should repress or oppose your ideas. It implies that you should be aware of your thoughts, label them, and let them flow through your mind without giving them any further attention.

Start encouraging good thoughts into your mind if you find that it's not flowing in that direction. Your brain will adjust through the previously described process when you become aware of and begin to align your thoughts to be positive.

2: Take in uplifting media

We have so many media available to us in this technological age. More print, electronic, and social media items are available now than at any other point in human history. Most of the time, we use all of this carelessly.

Everything that is provided to us is read or watched. We don't realize that the things we are exposed to in the media have a greater tendency than anything else to linger in our minds and impact our lives.

The media makes use of our exposure to advertising. The advertising impact persuades us that we are seeing what we want to experience by employing enticing and persuasive techniques. For this reason, you should exercise caution in accepting ideas that the media presents to you.

It goes without saying that it is impossible to cultivate a happy outlook if you constantly expose your mind to depressing material like sensationalist news articles, furious music, and scary movies.

Get exposed to some upbeat media: look for a humorous website, watch an inspirational film, listen to uplifting music, or read optimistic quotes (many websites provide these, and you can even discover inspiration on Facebook and Instagram). Purchase a video game console if you enjoy it. For individuals wishing to change their lives, MasteryTV.com is an excellent resource with a wealth of motivational and uplifting videos.

3: List Your Strengths and Convictions

Writing is one of the most effective ways to "inscribe" anything in your brain. Take out a piece of paper and list ten or more positive aspects of yourself. Write out ten or more positive aspects of your life as well.

After you're finished, place these lists by your bed and read them out loud each morning and evening before turning in for the night. You'll feel better and more confident the more you read and "drum" stuff into your head. This will cause your brain to perceive yourself differently if you are a chronic pessimist.

You can also list five or more things you are happy about daily. It might have been a comment you received at work or a discussion with an unknown person while out for a stroll in the afternoon. Putting it in writing and thinking about the good things will lift your spirits.

4: Surround Yourself with Positive People

Your identity is shaped by the individuals you spend most of your time with. You've heard your mother say that the people you spend time with shape who you become. Decide to hang out with upbeat folks. Even if you're trying to think positively, you might never be able to shift your mindset if everyone around you constantly says bad things. They might even tell you not to be optimistic or pursue personal development.

Let's say you want to think of yourself as a smart person, and everyone around you calls you stupid when you make a mistake, or you want to think of the world as a good place, and everyone talks about how hard life is.

Seek out inspiring people to motivate you. If you surround yourself with positive individuals, their energy will positively affect you and assist you in your mental transformation; if they reject negativity, you must do the same to blend in.

List at least five positive and inspiring persons you know from your neighborhood or employment. Jot down the qualities you wish to have in yourself that they have. Copy their admirable traits. To gain more knowledge from them and develop a friendship, try to get in touch with them and extend an invitation to lunch. Make sure to compliment them and express your admiration for them.

Following upbeat people on social media platforms like Twitter, Facebook, YouTube, and Instagram is also beneficial. Make sure to unfollow or conceal those who are unfavorable or whine constantly.

5: Make the most of it

Even if you think negatively, try to live a positive life. "Fake it till you make it," they say. Be gregarious, smile, congratulate others, and laugh even when you feel bad. David Schwartz asks readers to try this exercise from his book The Magic of Thinking Wide: "Try to feel defeated and smile big at the same time." It is not possible. A broad smile conveys self-assurance. That is a terrific experiment when you feel overwhelmed: "A big smile beats fear, rolls away worry, and defeats despondency." Make positivity your new normal. If you give it to the universe, it will be forced to return it to you. It will require a mental shift for your thinking to become the new self.

As we go over techniques to assist you in developing positive thinking, remember that using a technique alone won't make a difference in your life. The explanation above makes it clear that changing your thinking will take time and consistent practice over an extended period. Being optimistic is a lifelong skill that is acquired through daily practice. Now that you have returned or rewired your mind to think positively, let's get to the heart of developing positive thinking by discussing your actions to become more optimistic.

Chapter 5: Modify Your Mental Routines

Cognitive Behavioural Therapy

Many individuals have misgivings about counseling or therapy because they believe that "if I can't fix my problems, how is this person who barely knows me going to help?" However, in contrast to other types of therapy, this one truly promotes transformation.

A program that can fundamentally alter your thinking, whether you use it independently or with professional assistance. It's a way to make associations between ideas and actions and then, when needed, to appropriately sever those associations.

This book has previously touched on CBT a little bit. In this treatment, it was written that you were not an idiot, and we discussed the real issues that could lead someone to think that way about themselves since words have power. Incredible strength. Consider the distinction between comments like "you look stupid" and "you look silly" or even "you have a unique style." Consider that this compliment or criticism is being directed at you. The first is severe and cutting. Although much less, the second is still somewhat important. The third, however, is entertaining and guaranteed to make you chuckle. That is the force of language. Now, acknowledge that we are always conversing with ourselves. Our actions speak louder than our thoughts about it. Many people will accept this view of themselves even if they publicly deny it if someone has labeled them stupid for a long time and said they lack knowledge. They start to think of themselves as idiots, and frequently, they go to great lengths to conform to the perception of themselves as idiots. This is how frighteningly powerful negativity can be.

To solve this issue, you must...

Examine Your Ideas

What's happening within that? Are you aware? Can you recall what was going through your mind when you read the line above as you are reading this right now? And the paragraph that came before that?

You'll struggle with this if you're like most people. None is significant because their minds are constantly racing, bouncing from one thing to another. Usually, this is OK. The full ignorance of your inner world only returns to haunt you when negativity finds a place in your thinking.

Realizing that you are not your ideas is the first step towards change. You are not your ideas any more than you are your tongue canker or your thumbnail. Although it is a part of you, you are not who it is. After reading this book, you could have the impulse to become agitated whenever negativity appears. You might even get upset with yourself for finding it difficult to maintain your good attitude. But here's where the issue is. It's your mind, not yourself, that is struggling with positivity. That is the reason we are discussing positive thinking. Despite what many people think, you are not a thinker. Like any of your limbs or senses, your mind is just another tool at your disposal. Getting upset with yourself for not thinking positively is pointless, as you are not the one who is at fault. As the spectator, you are taking note.

That's who you are when you stop to observe the ideas that you are experiencing. Not the idea that results from that idea, criticizing it for being negative, but the observer seated behind it all and taking in the scene. It's who you are. You will also fight until you discover the stillness between the deluge of frantic ideas racing through your mind because it's similar to attempting to mentally levitate a key. You can't do it, why? Because you are attempting to compel something that isn't even related to you to obey you. Furthermore, you, the spectator, are not a part of your ideas. Finding the stillness behind the thoughts leads to peace, not trying to stop every thought.

The only reason you aren't thinking positively is that you focus too much on negative ideas.

An elderly, knowledgeable Native American man is said to have told his grandson the tale of the enormous black and white wolves within each of us. The white wolf symbolizes the virtuous, the true, and the honest. The destructive, dishonest, and evil are symbolized by the black wolf. When the wise man has finished narrating his tale, his grandson asks him, "Grandpa, which wolf wins?"The one you feed," the elderly guy then informs him.

We all have both positive and negative ideas going through our heads. Proceed and pay attention. There, not only can you hear them humming, but you can also feel their presence. Now, The trick is to focus more on those optimistic ideas than those pessimistic ones. The bad won't go away completely, and it shouldn't. It's not that negative thoughts are bad; the issue is that they control you.

Give Up

It takes practice, but so does talking and walking, and you probably did well with both. When an unfavorable thought comes to mind, ask yourself, "Is there anything I can do about this?"If so, try to determine what must be done and formulate a strategy. Decide when you need to start after you've prepared your action plan. Is it at this moment? Try letting go if not. If so, finish it now. Let go when you're done. Let go of the negative notion if you can do nothing about it.

"Letting it go": what does that mean? No, we won't be studying the Frozen lyrics. 'Let it Be' might be a better choice. It entails letting go of your responsibilities and moving forward. Therefore, if you think nobody likes you, consider asking yourself, "Is there anything I can do? And possibly there is. You may have made a mistake and should apologize to some individuals. That would be beneficial. Or maybe you think that people don't get you because they don't understand who you are. Fill them in, then. Look for avenues for self-expression. Ultimately, is there anything you can do to win everyone's approval? No. You must, therefore, let it go at the end of the day. Give it a go. Give up trying to change things right then and there and accept them as they are.

We run into problems when we cling on. In addition to making the past gloomy, holding onto the past causes us to miss the present and fear the future. Maybe you were harmed by a redhead a long time ago, so you're nervous around redheads now. You can, therefore, lose the opportunity to meet someone amazing if you shun them or reject them immediately. But what if you choose to ignore it? What if you let go of the past and leave it there, opening the potential that redheads from the past may not accurately reflect redheads from the present?

Though this is a ridiculous analogy, individuals do, in fact, frequently cling to items of this kind. Whether they be resentments based on age, gender, or sexual orientation, they may not enjoy some animals, the elements, or automobiles. They are clinging to their initial impressions and, for whatever reason, wish to resist the chance to form new ones, so they won't read works by authors they read twenty years ago.

However, consider what you could learn if you let it go. If you just let things go, imagine how your body and mind could develop and your emotional stability could strengthen. How do you let it go then? By restraining both the temptation to gaze forward and the need to look back. Concentrate on the here and now, as it is your only one. And it has been absent from you.

Techniques For Positive Thought That Are Fun And Relaxing

Don't squander your free time dwelling on the unpleasant and unfavorable events in your life. Rather, engage in constructive hobbies that make you happy and calm. You could utilize these suggestions to unwind in your spare time and lessen the tension in your life.

Let me also caution you that leisure time will not manifest completely. You must intentionally set aside a certain amount of time each day for this task. Taking some time to unwind—at least half an hour—is crucial for general well-being. Once you make this a habit, you'll notice a drastic shift in your outlook on life.

Read a book. You can read anything you like, but I advise you to avoid horror, morbidity, and unmotivating literature. It's best to read something inspirational. As you read the book, you ought to experience awe. I'm capable of doing this as well!"

I don't need to say more about music than Plato once. Turn on your preferred tunes, sit, and relish the sense of liberation and tranquility.

One great way to begin meditating is to pay attention to your breathing. Just pay attention to your breathing, to each inhale and exhale. Remember to breathe softly each time your thoughts stray from this goal. Inhale and exhale deeply. Avoid exerting yourself. Just be aware of your breathing. Each day, begin with 10 minutes and gradually extend it.

You will eventually reach a point during this exercise where your mind is clear of all thoughts if you practice this often and consistently! That's the magic you're going to seek! But that's over an extended period. Till then, relax and pay attention to your breathing gradually.

A stroll in the evening, a stroll in the morning, a little run or jog, or anything else that works for you will be OK. However, make physical activity a part of your daily schedule. The activity's production of pheromones can lift your mood.

Laugh: You might not be able to find humor in everything that happens to you, but there are probably a few things you can consider that will always make you smile. Recall those moments because it is impossible for unpleasant emotions to coexist with a joyful, smiling countenance.

Make something:

Engage in activities that will provide tangible products you may enjoy while relaxing.

If you enjoy cooking, prepare a meal for your family and friends and see how happy they are when they eat it.

Paint something if you enjoy painting.

You can sketch, color, and produce various paper crafts suitable for young children. You can do anything; your satisfaction from creating something will chase away the negative!

Techniques for having fun and relaxing are essential to living a more wholesome, contented, and joyful existence. These prevent bad thoughts from occurring. Enjoy them regularly to see a significant increase in your overall productivity.

Section Four

Feed the Monster Imaginary

The more attention you give those negative ideas, the more likely they will intensify and worsen. Consider that you are providing food for a terrifying monster! When you stop feeding and starve that monster, it will become tiny and lose its ability to control you. We have previously discussed the functioning of the subconscious mind. Once you have learned to control it, this may be your friend or the monster. Replace the negative thoughts that the monster in your head is feeding you with positive, energizing, and healthful ones to alter its behavior. When bad thinking arises, counter it with the following remedies:

Issue: I'm unable to complete the assignment my supervisor gave me.

Consider remedies rather than allowing it to rot in your head and feed the monster:

I could get an explanation from the boss.

I could assign the task to another person.

I could focus on finishing the task in a predetermined amount of time.

Your decision in these situations is based on why you cannot complete the task. For instance, relocate to an area free of distractions if there are excessive amounts of them. If you don't comprehend the task, asking for an explanation is the logical course of action. No matter how much you sit there feeling sorry for yourself, it won't get done. Give up giving in to your negative self-talk, or else the monster within will ruin your life.

You don't have to believe those anxious, frightening thoughts; they are just that—thoughts—and the more you attempt to ignore them and concentrate on them, the more real they become. Observe them vanish if you allow them to exist without causing trouble.

More of that will result from thoughts of anxiety, tension, dread, and uncertainty. For instance, I had an issue when I woke up this morning. My house's basement level was inundated. I could have stayed in bed and commiserated with myself. If I had done this, the water would have continued to seep into my carpets, worsening the situation. Even though I could see that other individuals were experiencing the same problem out of my window, I could have become terrified of the circumstances. An excessive quantity of worry would not solve the issue. I pushed away the useless ideas and tried to devise plans for myself and an elderly neighbor who was not as capable as I was. We collaborated and came up with answers, and rather than obsessing over the issue, we celebrated with a warm cup of tea and thanked ourselves for handling the situation. We refrained from feeding the pessimistic creature like the woman next door did. Three weeks from now, she will still be moping over the flood because she feeds the monster inside her and gets her kicks from spreading her toxic vibrations to everyone else. Don't be that individual. Be the person who solved the problem or the one who, despite its difficulty, believed that a solution existed.

The extent of what you allow the subconscious to accomplish is limited. Upon examining various religions from across the globe, you will discover that the most serene and content individuals seem to be Buddhist monks. They have nothing to their name. Why are they happy if they lead such a modest life? Instead of feeding the monster, they provide positive thoughts to their minds. They can embrace who they are in the scheme of things and turn off outside influences by practicing meditation, which enables them to accomplish that. We request that you alter your mental patterns, even if we do not ask you to don your saffron robes.

Practice starving the beast.

Locate a peaceful area where you can sit comfortably in a chair. Your hands should be in your lap. Make sure your back is straight and that your clothes are comfy. Inhale through your nostrils, and focus solely on your breathing. Don't think about anything else. Imagine it as an energy surge into your body. Feeling all negativity leave your head, hold your breath for a moment and then release it. Now close your eyes and repeat the exercise, focusing on your breathing and counting to seven while you inhale, holding your breath for five counts, and exhaling for eight. Imagine the force of the air entering your body and then the force of the air expelling all negative thoughts from your mind. Ignore all other thoughts. Forgive yourself and start over if you notice thoughts beginning to creep in. It will take some time before you start to see results because you are new at starving the monster. You'll get more energy and stop your thoughts from dwelling if you do this every day for 15 minutes. If it helps, surround yourself with things that inspire you. Perhaps while you're doing this, let the aromas of flowers help you relax. After completing this exercise, you'll have so much more energy. After you're done, take some time to relax and unwind since it lowers pulse rate and blood pressure. Then, get back to your hectic schedule.

Insight #8: Give Up Trying to Impress People and Compare Your Life to Theirs

Research on happiness has revealed that two major contributors to a miserable existence are attempting to impress everyone around you and comparing your life and yourself to others. These two behaviors must end immediately if happiness and success are your goals.

Why Is It So Hard for You to Impress People and Compare Yourself to Them?

You get the impression that you and your life are not good enough when you compare them to others. You begin identifying all the negative aspects of your life and ignore everything positive. This makes you feel terrible, and depression impairs your ability to think properly, increasing the chance that you will make poor judgments that will inevitably lead to failure in your life. Consequently, you must break this behavior permanently if you genuinely wish to be content and happy.

Furthermore, you must break the tendency of trying to impress others. Your life begins to revolve around other people, and you stop placing value on yourself when you start to become a people pleaser. You continue to move forward as long as people are content with you despite their mistreatment and usage of you. You may act as though everything is fine, but in reality, you are depressed. Consequently, you must address these two behaviors immediately to improve your life. Here are some actions to improve your satisfaction and gratification in life.

Give Up Frequently Using Social Media

The Happiness Research Institute conducted a Facebook experiment to find out how your habits and usage of social media affect your level of happiness. Half of the participants kept using Facebook as usual, and the other half stopped using it altogether for a week. The outcomes were astounding. They showed that, compared to those who had used Facebook during the study, the individuals who had managed to abstain from using the social media platform expressed greater satisfaction and enjoyment with their lives and with themselves. Furthermore, it demonstrated that regular Facebook users had 55 percent higher stress levels than non-users.

Because you see so many posts on various social media platforms about people "enjoying their life to the fullest and having a wonderful time," it is evident that frequent and constant usage of social media is bad for your emotional health. This gives you the impression that a lot is missing from your life, which depresses you. You must give up using social media excessively to be content with what you have. Reduce your weekly social media time by one hour to a maximum of ten minutes daily. You'll feel more at ease within if you use less.

Advice: If you find it difficult to resist the impulse to visit other social media platforms, you might choose to restrict your access to them, if only temporarily. The greatest apps to help with that include Self Control, StayFocusd, LeechBlock, and others. If you cut yourself off from social media, where it's easy to compare yourself to others, just try and see how it makes you feel after a few days.

Put Yourself First and Establish Limitations

The next thing you must realize is that you are the most important person in your life and require all your attention. Commit yourself that you will put yourself first before other people going forward. You must genuinely act on this belief. The next step is to establish limits on how much time you spend with other people. Reduce the time you used to spend helping your friends with their duties from five to three hours, and then add 30 minutes at a time. Furthermore, you have to be adamant about the limits you establish with them and decline to fulfill their requests if they coerce you. When you remain firm with someone, they gradually begin to back off.

Along with these actions, you must keep noting your blessings and giving them daily thanks. As a result, you'll become satisfied with your life, which will motivate you to quit comparing it to others.

Never Take Your Praise

Avoiding complacency is essential for personal development. Being satisfied indicates that you are aware of your needs. However, you can't get comfortable if you want to keep getting better. When you become complacent, you stop trying to get better. You may have experienced some success and, as they say, are basking in the glory of your previous achievements. The problem is that we don't live in the past; that is your history. Since change is the only constant in life, we constantly move in one direction. It is improbable that we will remain where we are if we do not proceed. Therefore, if we are not progressing, we are probably regressing and forfeiting our prior achievements.

Being complacent is letting up to the point of inaction. It is forfeiting growth in favor of cozy safety. Something about stability and comfort destroys us. The challenge is what keeps us relevant. A fish enterprise once caught fish in the ocean and transported them great distances. For the fish to stay fresh, they were maintained alive in aquariums. The fish just did not have the same flavor and texture as a newly caught fish when it got to its destination, which was the issue. Why? There were no predators in the tank to pose a threat to the fish while they were traveling. They were relaxed. Adding a few predators to each tank addressed the issue. The fish now had to remain vigilant during the journey, which improved the texture and flavor of the fish. What harm is complacency causing you now?

You Have 86400 Seconds

Making the most of your available time is a crucial part of living a life of mastery. One of your most valuable assets is your time.

The probability of your continued existence is known to Buddhists as your "precious incarnation." Your chances of being reincarnated are the same as if you tossed a life preserver into an ocean where a solitary turtle was swimming, and it popped up with its head in the middle on its first attempt. It is a miracle that you are still alive. You, your life, and your purpose are remarkable because of your incarnation's uniqueness. You are here for a reason.

There must be tasks you need to complete because you are here for a reason. However, there is an issue. The majority of people fall short of their potential. Most individuals never reach their full potential. For what reason is that the case? One of the biggest obstacles to our success is none other than ourselves! Yes, we put things off. Procrastination is an option. Nevertheless, biology also plays a role. Delaying tasks is also a habit. A lot of people have procrastination issues.

It's simple to achieve your goals when you know what has to be done. If you're unaware, you can learn the exact steps to success through blogs, books, seminars, and lectures. Every year, people set routines, businesses implement programs, and we all make resolutions to improve our lives and eventually achieve our goals. What, then, is the issue? The issue lies in procrastination, which is a habit. It is breakable, just like any other habit we may have.

Let's briefly examine the mechanics of procrastination. How do we put things off?

What actions should we take, when should we take them to achieve success, and why do we take them?

When we put anything off, what do we do? What does delaying get us in return? Some will check their email, browse the internet, read articles online, watch a movie, text for hours, or engage in other distracting activities. Determining what you do when you put things off is not difficult. We will be reviewing these exercises in a moment, so take a moment to consider them. After you've worked out "what you do," we can discuss "why you do these things."

So, what motivates you to carry out these actions? This is the element of reward. There must be some sort of reward since you get nothing out of it. Your activities are typically enjoyable, engaging, simple, or fulfilling. These "rewards" serve to strengthen the procrastinating habit. This explains why quitting procrastination can be so difficult.

How, then, do we get away? Do we push ourselves? Will pushing oneself result in the same benefits as putting off doing something? Not very likely. Force is disagreeable and doesn't interact with our innate rewards-based learning mechanism. What then functions? We need to recognize the benefits of not putting off tasks and criticize the things that cause us to put them off.

We can evaluate the activities that cause us to put things off by examining their costs or other unpleasant aspects. What would it cost to spend a whole day instead of working on Facebook or watching movies on YouTube? You are aware that it takes up time, an extremely valuable resource. But would this information be sufficient to break your procrastinating habit?

Inquiring about the motivations behind our actions can be gratifying in and of itself. Think about your feelings while you are inquisitive. It is inherently satisfying to be curious. Brewer advises against pushing ourselves to cease procrastinating when it occurs. Rather, just be interested and aware of the reasons behind your actions. What are the advantages and disadvantages of this behavior?

Accepting The Variations

People often shy away from me when I mention "self-love" because it's not a notion they understand. They consider it self-serving and believe that others should come before themselves. But how can you be the best version of yourself for the people you love if you don't like who you are? I have a funny tale about this that I can tell you. A long time ago, I used to let other people dictate what I wore. It wasn't as though I required their influence. It was because I was led to believe that I required their influence by others. Then, I became aware of something. I had to ask for their approval if I dressed in a way that would please other people. This erodes your integrity and makes you value other people's opinions more highly than your sense of self.

One of the girls I worked with helped me realize this. Regardless of her attire, she consistently exuded style. You may attribute this to her fortunate physique, but that wasn't the case. It took me some time to figure out that it was something far more significant than that. You don't need anyone else's approval if you are content with what you are wearing. Because of the level of confidence YOU generate, you shine. What you wear is not important. It all comes down to having self-confidence in your identity. No one else's approval is necessary if you wear that dress with the self-assurance that you look wonderful and will look fantastic no matter what you decide to wear.

Spending some time observing individuals might be beneficial. Their level of self-love determines their manner of being. Regardless of their size, they exude confidence and look fantastic because, instead of the fancy names on their clothes, their confidence and body language speak volumes. Put on clothes that fit you. The world will accept you for who you are as an individual if it makes you happy.

Long ago, before I knew anything about loving oneself, I had close friends who had just tied the knot. One thing stood out each time they went to a gathering or supper. They had numerous arguments. I knew them better than this, and I knew they were incredibly in love with one another, but many saw this as a sign of discord in the marriage. A strong feeling of self was what caused them to dispute. If they had a belief in something, neither of them gave in. You must understand that YOU are not required to adopt the viewpoints of others. You are entitled to your own opinions. Naturally, there can be a good amount of compromise, but if friends or a partner are causing you misery, you must accept your differences and let them know you think differently. It's acceptable to have different desires. You can express your opinions. Being attractive is not necessary for loving oneself, but loving oneself means not being scared of your principles.

There's no need to act rudely the next time someone tries to make arrangements without first contacting you. Just say you're not working on this. You lose your sense of self when you give in and let other people walk all over you, making you quite pessimistic about life. You should never be scared to speak about what's best for you while experiencing self-love. Kelly detested the evening when her spouse returned with his friends to watch sports. She didn't even enjoy sports, and they treated her like a slave. She eventually realized she could use this as an opportunity for a night out. She just told her husband that she had things she wanted to do while making sandwiches ahead of time. She was happier as a result, and soon, he was too. It's not the only thing in a relationship to fulfill people's expectations of you. It's all about doing what's best for you, and Kelly felt more confident the first time she could urge her spouse to acknowledge that she had feelings as well. Accept the distinctions between you. You are unique from other people. You are a unique person with unique decisions.

Make sure that your actions in life are ultimately beneficial to YOU, even if you must compromise. If you don't, you become more and more resistant to life and begin to resent the chances you lost because you catered to the opinions of others. Reclaim the self-assurance that initially drew others to you by being true to yourself. Nothing is different. You still can be the star of your show, but sometimes, you have to learn to say "no" to life and accept that this is okay.

Chapter 4: Strategies for Becoming a Positive Thinker and Overcoming Negative Thoughts

Although an optimist is aware of life's realities, they prefer to concentrate their energies on the positive aspects of it. It's like deciding between a half-full or half-empty glass—it's a matter of mindset.

You will learn about several actions that are not easy, especially at first, but you can accomplish it! The more you practice positive thinking, the more ingrained it will become in your mindset. You will have to make this conscious choice every day, but there is no other way to improve your lot in life. This is relevant to the mental, social, and psychological aspects in addition to the physical ones.

The following are some strategies for getting rid of negative thoughts and developing good ones:

Tip #1: Honestly assess yourself. This can be achieved through meditation or some alone time. You need to recognize where your regular negative ideas originate from. You need to identify precisely which aspect of your life is negatively impacted by your negative thoughts. Is it your job, personal connection, or how you look? Once it's recognized, you need to take another look at it and consider whether criticizing yourself or dwelling on the bad aspects of the circumstance would assist in resolving any problems. Consider whether your pessimistic ideas are making things better or worse. The following action is vital if your response is negative. You need to come up with a plan on how to turn things around. Thinking positively demands action, not just giving up and moping about a circumstance. You will probably notice the results as you start practicing the required tasks, motivating you to keep going.

It's not about growing an ego; rather, it's about having faith in your ability to better yourself and achieve your goals.

Tip #2: Silence the naysayers in your head. You need to be aware of your feelings and ideas when doing this. You need to catch yourself when you start to believe the negative voice in your head that says you are unworthy and will never succeed. Then, you need to meditate once more and look at the bright side of things. Creating affirmations to counter the negative ideas you are contemplating is another tactic. Swap out "I can't" with "I will." Speak less of words like tension, anger, depression, jealousy, etc., and more of words like contentment, serenity, love, motivation, etc. Remember that ideas translate into words and deeds.

Recall that this is an issue of self-control and choices. Refuse to listen to the voice that wants you to feel anxious, useless, and without hope. You are aware of your ability. All you need to do to overcome the obstacles in life is take initiative.

Tip #3: Ask for Help – Asking for professional or family support is always a good idea, especially if you are going through significant emotional breakdowns, insecurities, or other unpleasant feelings that are pushing you toward self-destruction. A professional can also guide you toward heart and mind healing while helping you discover the source of your actions or bad beliefs. Yes, you are the first to need to make a change, but sometimes it can be really helpful to acknowledge that you have an issue, understand how serious it is, and talk to someone you can trust about it. Sometimes, all we need to improve is a second set of eyes to reassure us.

Tip #4: Practice self-affirmation. Although we typically want to hear affirmations from others and even use their opinions to define ourselves, we also need to be rooted in the knowledge that we are valuable individuals who know who we are. We occasionally need to tell ourselves, "I can do this! I can do it!" -- If you say it with conviction over and over, even when you don't truly think you can, you'll quickly believe that you can. Own a mantra or "magic" statement of your own. It can "trick" your mind into believing it. You can write down the good thought or say it in addition to repeating it.

Tip #5: Focus on your sense of worth. Even if they project confidence, some people harbor deep self-doubt. Sometimes, you have to present a confident image, so while waiting for that chance, make sure you're doing everything possible to increase your self-worth. Positivity about yourself will assist you in getting rid of any potential negativity. The following methods and exercises will assist you in developing this aspect:

There won't be any discussion of negative self-perception in this activity. All you need to do is list your accomplishments, no matter how big or small, along with your positive attributes (don't be bashful). Additionally, you may invite your loved ones to add to the list and just acknowledge the accuracy of what they have written. Then, READ it frequently, particularly if you're having a bad day. Not your failures or worries should define you, but these things.

An additional practice is to create a "self-esteem checklist."Just jot down some simple acts that might bring you joy, then resolve to do them more frequently. Or, to be even more precise, make it a daily goal to do at least one task from the list. You are teaching your mind that you can accomplish your goals by doing this.

Additionally, you can concentrate on your flaws so that they might someday turn into strengths.

Sixth tip: Always give it your all. By giving it your all, you'll feel good about yourself and help to strengthen your sense of self-worth. Let's say you have a presentation at work. It might only be covered in your routine meeting. On the other hand, if you put up your best effort in your presentation, you will feel confident in it, and others will, too. If you obtain positive feedback, don't be shocked by it (jot it down!). This will boost your confidence even more.

Tip #7: Get your body moving! Physical activity and exercise that involves movement can lift your spirits. They will help us declutter and bolster our confidence so we can overcome any obstacles that may arise.

The eighth tip is to cultivate thankfulness. Everyone should do this to adopt a more positive outlook. It takes practice to properly acknowledge and value life's blessings. Why? Your optimism and sense of contentment will grow due to your thankfulness. With so much to be grateful for, why choose to be unhappy, melancholy, or agitated?

Let's attempt this easy task. Create a "list of gratitude." Simply write down everything that makes you happy or that you are grateful for in life—even the little things, like the stunning sky that appears to be a flawless canvas. Keep adding items to the list. At the end of the exercise, you will undoubtedly conclude that life is wonderful and that negative notions shouldn't enter your mind.

How To Disengage Yourself From Negative Thoughts Mentally

First, realize that negativity is permeating your daily experiences, even though it can sometimes be difficult to notice.

It wasn't until a friend made that observation that I realized how pessimistic my thinking was. I had previously assumed that thinking negatively was common. But in the end, I did come to terms with the idea that, in a sense, I was the negative elephant in the room. I was able to change my outlook altogether once I came to terms with that thought. I decided to mentally confront negativity if I wanted my life to change.

Since "you are what you eat," as the cliché goes, I changed how I ate. I only ate fast food before my transition, largely because it was practical. However, it also had a bad impact on my physical health. Changing your eating habits is one of the simplest methods to start changing your life if you are trying to repair your negative ideas.

I don't know about you, but I always feel awful after eating bad food. Imagine the impact on your emotional state every day if your body reacts negatively to food. Changing your dietary habits may seem ridiculous, but since your body is your temple, you should treat it with the same respect as if it were a pricey prize from the fair. That's not to suggest you buy only organic food, but you should probably quit putting unhealthy things in your body that aren't doing it any good. Making dietary changes is one of the best methods to begin your journey into the positive zone. You feel more confident since you can now recognize the nasty entity constantly taking credit for your accomplishments.

Chapter 8: Reaching the Positive Atmosphere

Congratulations! You've made it to the happy place where negativity is no longer tolerated.

Your bad ideas and their companions Doubt, Fear, and Negativity are now seated on the other side of the door. At first, the positive zone can be frightening, but if you are willing to consider altering your thinking, you will ultimately transform your entire outlook.

I still recall how quickly I rejected this zone the first time I entered it. I had closed my mind to the possibility of change. Until then, I was content and ignorant of my nasty nature. I have changed over the years, but everyone is unique. So, how can we fully implement a 180-degree positive thought shift? Above all, you need to be prepared to accept the constructive thoughts, challenges, and ideas that will be thrown your way. Negative ideas and thoughts will always be present in our minds; it is just a fact of life. However, how you rearrange these ideas and thoughts will change your outlook on it.

Methods For Retraining Your Mind

1) De-stress fully by turning off your phone, going to a quiet spot, lighting a few candles, and practicing daily meditation. Although there are many other kinds of mediation, I have included the following few:

1) Meditation with guidance
2) Unrestricted Awareness
3) Consciousness
4) Mindfulness

Please go to: for additional details on these styles of meditation.

Many different types of meditation, including yoga, prayer, and other mental health practices, help you release tension. Painting is also a fantastic meditation method because it lets you express your feelings. You can also examine all of those uncertainties and conflicting feelings. Painting doesn't require artistic talent; you only need to pick up a brush and manipulate the paint with your hands.

It's sometimes in moments of defeat that the best work is produced. In addition to being a potent healer, music also lets people's imaginations wander to nicer places. A book, a magazine, or online literature are excellent alternatives to lessen those stressors.

2) If necessary, limit your use of social media even though social media is now the standard. Since the first social media website was launched in 1997, social media is still a relatively new idea. Two more significant platforms decided to join the social party in 2004-05. Social media has taken over our lives in the same way that a tsunami might submerge a small community. Decompress after a demanding workday for amusement, to interact with others, to share knowledge, etc. Nonetheless, a plethora of research has connected social media to sadness, discontent, and divorce in the majority of cases.

Despite the seemingly innocuous nature of this social pleasure, social media impacts every part of our existence. Nowadays, anything can be accessed with just a push of a button. In my opinion, social media presents these concepts or beliefs, which aren't always applicable to everyone. One begins to compare one's life to other people's when one spends endless hours on social media platforms, which can be highly risky. At that point, smiling photos of amicable couples are just that—pictures. These people occasionally only display to society what they wish to be viewed. But you never truly see what's going on behind the scenes, like the foreclosed signs on the front lawn, the mounting debt, or the cheating spouse who constantly comes up with new reasons. People will never display the true cinematic preview of their lives on these social media platforms. A tale always has two sides; although someone's life may appear ideal, the true action starts when the computer shuts down and the keyboard is switched off.

Some refer to it as a 30, 60, or 90-day social detox; giving up social media is entirely voluntary. Nonetheless, research indicates that merely cutting back on social media usage can boost an individual's happiness by about 80%. Try spending more time with family or friends in person instead of wasting it on social media.

3) Another excellent method for removing negative ideas from your mind and enhancing your attractiveness is to exercise. It also lessens stress because you are actively busy, and your mind is less focused on other things. I hate to break the news to you, but using the television remote control does not qualify as exercise. Exercise methods that bring you joy include getting off the sofa, hiking, playing sports, taking nature walks, and even doing housework.

My coworker A.W. reported that his confidence had significantly increased due to his weight loss. He was an emotional eater before he gained weight; the more food he consumed, the happier he felt. His comfort and affection were food. He developed health troubles as a result of his enormous weight, which prompted further complications. He made eating well and losing weight his way of life. If you want to change your unfavorable influences, I strongly advise exercising.

4) Concentrating on the negative things you say about yourself and transforming them into positive ideas is a terrific method to empower yourself and refocus your thoughts. I try to think of at least one encouraging remark or phrase to tell myself daily. You can even write yourself a letter of encouragement or jot down some good thoughts on sticky notes to hang on your wall. Writing these thoughts down will enable you to say them aloud every day. This is

empowering, in my opinion, as it teaches you to be a rock star in your imagination and learn to love yourself more. Being confident comes from loving who you are and eliminating the desire to seek approval from others. Self-empowerment aims to enable your inner confidence enhancer to overcome those self-defeating ideas.

5) A wonderful approach to start your day is with a daily affirmation. They uplift you and fortify your state of mind. A few years back, a high school student was one of the inspirational guest speakers at a business conference I attended. Nobody has spoken so elegantly as I have heard at such a young age. She wrote and repeated an affirmation to herself daily, which was one of the secrets to her success. She followed her words as they led her past all the weeds growing in her way. I eventually came up with my daily affirmation, which I tell myself since it helps me feel good about myself, boosts

my confidence, and fortifies my thinking. Here are a few quotes I use to remind myself of this daily.

The Power of Meditation to Calm Your Mind

Around the world, many people meditate both before and after their workday. It is a technique for mental calmness, eliminating unfavorable ideas, and overall learning to be more "present" in day-to-day living. Using this technique, you may assist your mind in becoming clear of negative thoughts so that positive ones can take root.

Affirmations and imagery, the next two ideas you'll study, are closely related to meditation. In certain cases, you can begin your day with meditation and then use the next two techniques as a beneficial approach to begin your day. All of this can be completed in less than 15 to 30 minutes, significantly improving your mental health!

Methods for Meditation

The correct approach to meditation is covered in many books and reference materials. You may always locate a more in-depth book, audiobook, or eBook to assist you in learning the correct approach to meditation. This easy workout is the best place to start.

Locate a spot where you can sit and relax without worrying about anything for a short while. This may be your den, workplace, bedroom, or even outside (if you live in a quiet neighborhood). The majority of people meditate while seated, such as in an Indian manner, but the most important thing is to make sure you are comfortable. Now close your eyes and focus just on inhaling. Let go of any other thoughts that may come to mind.

At the very least, try this for five minutes each day, and as you get more comfortable, attempt longer. It will be difficult for you to do this at first, but you will soon appreciate the practice and feel much better about yourself when you are in the moment!

Installing the free app "Headspace," accessible on the Google Play and iTunes app stores, can be a good idea for more practice. Using a series of 10-minute activities, this smartphone app will walk you through the principles of meditation.

Exercise Suggestion: Commit to meditating for five minutes every day, preferably right after you get up. As you can, increase the length of your sessions gradually.

Techniques For Happiness

Who wouldn't want to be happy? When life presents an opportunity to enjoy life to the fullest, no one would allow themselves to be lonely. Our purpose is to live it to the fullest and with abundance. For most people, happiness may be illusively close. You may be someone who has experienced a great deal of grief and disappointment and who has become accustomed to seeing loneliness and misery as natural as day and night. As a result, we look for happiness with the wrong people and in the wrong places.

In any case, why does it matter? Is having the ideal, well-paying work not sufficient? Is it wrong to accept an excellent partner who does not provide you happiness? Is contentment too highly valued?

Conversely, happiness dramatically increases a person's chances of success in any effort they undertake. Research indicates that happy doctors diagnose patients more accurately and efficiently and may instil optimism in their patients. Schools that place a greater emphasis on their children's social and emotional development typically see increases in academic achievement and behavioural improvements. Happier individuals are more inclined to be willing to reach out and assist one another, as well as make more beneficial contributions to society. They are more inclined to vote, volunteer, and build a strong community.

Since happiness is what we ultimately want out of life, it is really important. Even though it gets neglected too frequently, our subconscious gives it more weight than any material. Take note of these tactics that could give your life a boost if you wish to start along the path to happiness:

Establishing your objective

Knowing what you want and working toward it is the first step in achieving true happiness. Nothing is more effective than establishing specific objectives and outlining the necessary measures. Your blood will race as you anticipate anything, such as realizing a specific dream, and you will become enthused about all the opportunities. A spark of anticipation may ignite in our minds as we consider all the goals we have set for ourselves. You will feel more purposeful and meaningful when you have something to aim for. Having a goal helps you be accountable and responsible for the direction you want your life to take. In the middle of all the chaos in the world, having a goal would help you stay grounded and calm, just like a compass would always tell you where the north is.

Be clear about your objectives. Whether it's a major weight loss or that European tour, it matters not—what matters is that you be explicit when you set your goals. It would be much easier to get back on track when you sense your focus waning if you have something specific and tangible to concentrate on. Knowing what you truly desire will enable you to focus all your efforts on achieving that specific objective. This implies that you would avoid wasting time on things that are not as crucial or relevant to reaching that goal and would make the greatest use of all you have related to it. A basic example would be to forgo your third Starbucks coffee of the day and save the cash for the trip of a lifetime. Purchasing nutritious food rather than junk and processed food will undoubtedly help you achieve your weight loss objectives.

Divide your objectives into manageable parts. When you consider completing a job to achieve your goal, try not to get carried away. Maybe your priority should be to lose five pounds a month if you want to wear a size six bikini this summer. By breaking down a goal, you can prevent yourself from becoming overly anxious or discouraged that you won't be able to accomplish it. You will experience a sense of accomplishment when you accomplish these minor objectives, inspiring you to keep going and go above and beyond. Perhaps an extra ten pounds next month will go toward your ideal getaway—a little more than five pounds. Furthermore, it would be simpler to fix mistakes and start over.

Vision Board and Motivational Instrument

Did you realize that visual stimuli might cause our brains to respond more favourably? For instance, you know what red looks like because you have already studied it in school. You know that red elicits strong feelings, such as love, rage, or hatred. But why does receiving an email with a red font in the subject line make us angry or uneasy? An image can elicit feelings in the viewer that words alone could never. You may use the same idea for your objectives. Having grandiose dreams and aspirations in your brain is one thing, but putting them in writing is quite another. So, how is a vision board made?

Spend some time planning and outlining your objectives. It would encourage you to move toward them with greater assurance. Additionally, it helps you regain focus when you become sidetracked by surrounding stimuli.

Unwind and enjoy yourself. Making a vision board, sometimes called a life collage, is a good way to align your soul and intellect in the right direction. Avoid overstressing yourself, particularly if you are not an innate artist. Now is not the time to attempt to force those pictures into your life; instead, discover your flow and enjoy yourself while doing this.

Go go crazy with your creativity. When you write down a specific objective, support it with images, quotations, uplifting words, and visual affirmations. Make the most of the pictures you use; everything that motivates you to accomplish your objective should be pinned on your board. Allow your passion for realizing your ideas to inspire your creativity, but keep the board in mind. When you're done, hang this up somewhere noticeable in your room or workstation. This way, even when life gets busy, it reminds you of your mission.

Modifying your perspective

Pursuing your objectives and finding happiness are closely related to altering your perspective. You will discover that pursuing your aspirations will involve many obstacles and difficulties that will try to bring you down. One must have an optimistic outlook to truly persevere and achieve any goal. Though it could take some time to shift one's perspective, being purposeful and trying to see the positive side of things will get you closer to your objective.

Strive to overcome your fear. The greatest obstacle to real happiness is this. You will undervalue yourself and accept mediocrity if you give in to fear. You would get tunnel-visioned and miss out on greater chances available to you.

Cherish yourself.

Even though it can be the simplest step toward pleasure, liking oneself can be difficult to achieve. Sometimes, as long as someone else's shortcomings do not reflect poorly on us, it is simpler to accept their own. We lavishly shower others with presents, spend time with them, and prioritize their needs over our own. While this isn't necessarily bad, you should reassess your priorities if you find yourself losing yourself while making other people happy. Giving away what you don't have an abundance of is impossible. Thus, remember that you are worthy of love and care as well.

Recognize how you feel and respond to different circumstances. Pay attention to your instincts, and don't discount or disregard your natural reactions. Being self-aware will help you better understand who you are and make it easier for you to show love to others.

Self-love should not be confused with self-worship. To love oneself is acknowledging your strengths and shortcomings while focusing on your strong points. Self-love is acknowledging that you are human and that mistakes are to be expected rather than implying that you are superior to other people. It entails having complete regard for oneself.

Chapter X. Fostering Appreciation and Gratitude

We may consider gratitude to be a small or unimportant emotion. Saying "thanks" to someone who has assisted us or given us a present is one way to show our appreciation. But thankfulness is a strong feeling that can improve our lives significantly. Developing an attitude of thankfulness and appreciation can enhance our general well-being, help us acknowledge the numerous benefits in our lives, and strengthen our resilience in trying times.

One of the main advantages of practising thankfulness is that it can assist us in turning our attention from negativity to positivity. It's normal to become engrossed in depressing thoughts or feelings when feeling tense, nervous, or overwhelmed. We may dwell on the things we lack, the problems in our lives, or the things we wish were different. But when we set out to be thankful for what we already have, we start to have a new perspective on the world. Suddenly, the things we used to gripe about or take for granted look like priceless gifts.

Strengthening our sense of resilience can also be achieved via practising appreciation and thankfulness. When confronted with obstacles, failures, or disappointments, feeling dejected or disheartened is a common reaction. However, we can cultivate a more optimistic attitude on life by consciously thinking back on the things we are thankful for. This implies that we can better manage the challenging emotions that accompany challenging circumstances, but it does not imply that we ignore or dismiss them. We are more likely to overcome adversity and discover happiness and purpose when grounded in a solid foundation of appreciation and gratitude.

How might we develop appreciation and thankfulness in our daily lives? Establishing a thankfulness practice is one method. Just spending a few minutes daily thinking about the things you must be grateful for can accomplish this. Another thing you may do is develop the habit of thanking people in your immediate vicinity, such as friends, family, and coworkers.

By engaging in mindfulness exercises, one can also foster appreciation and thankfulness. We are more likely to notice the small things that make us happy and grateful when we are present in the moment. We often miss innumerable tiny moments of beauty and wonder, such as the flavour of your favourite cuisine, the feel of the sun on your skin, or the sound of a loved one laughing. By engaging in mindfulness practices and purposefully observing these instances, we can cultivate a more profound appreciation for our environment.

Lastly, it's critical to keep in mind that gratitude is a skill we can actively develop in our interpersonal interactions as well as something we feel. By showing our appreciation to people in our community, we strengthen our bonds with them and spread kindness throughout the globe. By cultivating appreciation and thankfulness, we may enhance our well-being and make the world more compassionate and pleasant for everyone.

Techniques to Get Rid of Procrastination

First of all,

It's normal to feel overwhelmed and demotivated during trying times. Procrastination can become a major obstacle to achievement, keeping people from accomplishing their objectives and triumphing over hardship. On the other hand, procrastination may be overcome, and the motivation to pursue success may be rekindled by utilizing practical tactics.

1. Establish Specific Objectives:

Establish meaningful objectives that are precise and unambiguous for yourself first. Having a clear idea of what you want to do makes it simpler to stay motivated and focused, which lowers the tendency to put things off.

2. Divide Up the Tasks:

Big jobs can frequently appear overwhelming and intimidating, which makes people put them off. Divide difficult activities into smaller, more doable segments. You can keep your sense of progress and prevent overwhelm by concentrating on one step at a time.

3. Establish a Timetable:

Create a well-organized timetable that lists your daily tasks and due dates. You may establish Accountability and a sense of urgency by giving jobs defined time windows. To form a productive habit, try your best to adhere to your timetable.

4. Set goals and assign tasks:

Determine which tasks are most important to your success and rank them in order of importance. Assign duties that are capable of being completed by others so that you can concentrate on the parts of your journey that are most important. By doing this, you not only save time but also lessen the chance of putting things off.

5. Take Away Distractions:

Acknowledge the distractions that often impede your development, such as social media, too much television, or an untidy workstation. Reduce these interruptions by setting up a workspace that encourages productivity. To focus, consider arranging your workstation, disabling notifications, or utilizing productivity tools.

6. Determine Accountability

Seek the assistance of a buddy, mentor, or accountability partner who can assist in keeping you on course. Consistent feedback and check-ins can help you overcome procrastination and maintain motivation.

7. Honor Advancement:

Celebrate and acknowledge your progress along the road. Rewarding yourself for reaching goals helps you stay motivated and promote good behaviour. Treating yourself to something you enjoy or taking a break to unwind and refresh can be small celebrations.

In summary:

Procrastination can be a big challenge during difficult circumstances, but you can overcome it with the appropriate tactics. You may keep the drive to overcome obstacles and succeed by setting clear goals, breaking down chores, making a timetable, prioritizing, eliminating distractions, finding Accountability, and celebrating accomplishments. Never forget that you can overcome procrastination and realize your full potential with endurance and drive. It is never too late to start.

Developing Self-Assurance and Eliminating Self-Doubt

It is essential to develop self-confidence and eradicate self-doubt throughout difficult situations. These two elements are crucial to our drive to succeed and overcome challenges. This chapter will examine practical methods for igniting our inner fire, finding inspiration, and cultivating a resilient mindset to get us through whatever obstacle life throws.

Confidence in one's values, talents, and abilities is known as self-confidence. It is the cornerstone around which success is constructed. But difficult circumstances frequently cause our confidence to waver, so we must actively work to build and reinforce it. Recognizing our accomplishments, no matter how minor they may seem, is one method to do this.

The use of constructive self-talk is another effective strategy for building self-esteem. Our inner monologue has a big influence on our thoughts and behaviour. We may rewire our mental patterns and increase our confidence by substituting positive affirmations for negative ones. Remind yourself of your advantages, see yourself succeeding, and tell yourself, "I am capable, resilient, and worthy of success."

It is equally crucial to remove self-doubt as it is to have self-confidence. To overcome self-doubt, fighting negative thoughts and replacing them with empowering beliefs is imperative. Self-doubt is the voice that whispers, "You can't do it" or "You're not good enough." While doubt is common, it does not define your skills or potential. Embrace activities that increase your self-worth, ask loved ones for assistance, and surround yourself with good influences.

Furthermore, overcoming self-doubt requires accepting failure as a necessary step toward achievement. Adopt a growth mindset in which failures are seen as opportunities for learning and uncertainty is converted into resolve.

When faced with hardship, it's normal to feel demotivated and think about giving up. But we can find the will to keep going if we work on removing self-doubt and developing self-confidence. Recall that obstacles are a necessary part of the path and that success does not come easily. Remain optimistic, stay focused, and never give up.

Effectively Combating Negative Ideas

You are likely so caught up in your negative thoughts that you are having trouble recognizing them and learning how to get past them. It's critical to learn how to deal with negative thoughts because, if you don't, your negativity may develop a dysfunctional thought pattern. In the worst-case scenario, negative thinking can cause medical problems such as the collapse of bodily systems as you lose the will to live, as well as mental disorders such as depression. Recognize your negative ideas and quickly replace them with productive, positive ones to combat them. Your perseverance, commitment, and tenacity are required; the rewards will be well worth it.

Unfavourable Thought Patterns

Various primary forms of negative thinking can be recognized and explained as follows: -

Individualization

This is called holding a pity party by some and playing the victim by others. In any case, personalizing addresses the issue of blaming yourself for bad things that happen to you or even things that don't happen to you daily.

sifting

When you intentionally search for the negative in everything and decide to ignore the many positives that should be taken into account, you are engaging in a negative thought habit. Positive events are considered anomalies, and you attempt to justify their non-importance.

polarization

You perceive things in black or white when you polarize a scenario. This restricts your options for reaction because you will categorize things as nice or terrible. You decide not to think about the different gradations of grey or possible reasons for the situation.

Becoming catastrophic

Catastrophizing is the next negative thought habit in which you constantly assume the worst. You approach situations with the conviction that you will not succeed and that your actions are not a good idea.

Oversimplification

This occurs when you imagine that there will be a never-ending cycle of pessimistic thinking if something goes wrong. Your entire world will end suddenly, and everything will become a disaster.

You will discover that you have engaged in all four of these harmful thought patterns when you read through them at some point in your life. Maybe you still possess them. Negative thought patterns will impact your capacity to proceed positively, but now that you've recognized them, you can attempt the following to change them.

Your Body and Negative Thoughts

Negative ideas have an impact on your body in addition to your mind. This is due to research showing that negative ideas tend to originate in your brain's most rudimentary region. The amygdala is the brain region that triggers your fight-or-flight reaction in the event of a threat. It responds swiftly to imaginative alterations in your physical form. Your body may tense, your breathing may quicken, your blood pressure may fluctuate, your heart may race, or your body temperature may rise while you think negatively.

Even with the information in this chapter, if you still have trouble recognizing your negative thoughts, you can watch your body's reaction.

Getting Rid of Negative Thoughts

Try this exercise before continuing. Enter a dimly lit, peaceful space where you know you won't be bothered or distracted by outside noise. You can set a timer for the ten minutes you must spend in the room. Breathe deeply as you attempt to rid your mind of the day's ideas. You must now practice mindfulness and learn to listen to rather than ignore your mind.

Your inner voice will start talking and say the most random things. Ask why you are performing this exercise, or remind you of things you haven't done. That's how you talk to yourself; let yourself listen to what it says. Are you speaking kind things to yourself that make you feel better? After hearing your inner voice, do you feel horrible? What feelings are you experiencing?

If you have been observing, you will also notice that your breathing goes shallower and faster as your thoughts become more negative. Decide which negative thought pattern is present at this point. Pay attention to your inner voice and respond to arguments with reason and logic. Tell your inner voice that you are eating better meals and that you are prepared to be patient to see long-lasting results if it tells you that you are overweight and will never amount to anything.

Perform this action for each negative idea you have for the next ten minutes. After the timer sounds, you'll feel better, more confident, and upbeat.

Furthermore, you should consider whether your negative beliefs are based on reality or if your active imagination is to blame for their development. Imagine your friend telling you what's going through your mind. Which counsel would you offer your friend? You'll discover that even if you've been criticizing yourself, you will find it upsetting if someone else did anything similar to a loved one.

Give up thinking negative thoughts; they are bad for your mental well-being and your relationships with those around you. Refrain from letting your thoughts warp what is genuine.

Chapter 2: A Great Duty

Do you know you are the only one in charge of your life? No one else, not even your spouse, family, teacher, or coach, can hold you accountable for what you do in life.

The existence of a tiny thinker is one in which others shoulder all the responsibilities. They received poor advice from their guidance counsellor in high school, which cost them a useless degree. They spend whatever money they have without thinking about the consequences since their parents never taught them how to create a budget. The question is, who is ultimately accountable for your life? Those claims may be true—one investor may have lost all his money due to bad stock advice, or an unreliable business partner may have stolen your wonderful concept and made millions of it.

When a small-minded individual places blame on someone else, they give that person more authority to make decisions. They don't make decisions that benefit the small Thinker because they don't care about the other person or situation; instead, they make decisions that serve their interests. Put another way, when the little Thinker abdicates responsibility for their actions, they lose any power to influence the world around them.

Consider this: when someone apologizes, who do you regard more? Will you forgive someone who says, "I'm sorry I yelled at you, but I was hungry, upset about my mother, and frustrated because of my tax problems?" or "I'm sorry for what I did; it was uncalled for, and there was no excuse, please forgive me?"

You can likely distinguish between the two types of apologies. One is sincere, admits to the error, and places no blame elsewhere. The goal of the second apology is to absolve oneself of any accountability for the actions. That justification wouldn't hold water, would it? Naturally, no!

Let's continue the apologies analogy for a little while longer. The initial apologies lacked justification. "I apologize; I did something improper and that was wrong." Should those remarks have been authentic, the offender must have acknowledged their mistake. Then, in addition to apologizing, people might also examine themselves to determine the source of their actions.

Someone who assumes responsibility is a Big Thinker. Taking responsibility for the mistake and delving within to see what went wrong. This is a big-thinking act. The tiny Thinker never learns from their mistakes because they shift the blame to another person or situation. Saying something like, "I'm sorry I yelled, but I was hungry," won't make a little thinker change their mind because all they're doing is looking for an escape from accountability.

So why do dimwits act in that way? Since it's more convenient than accepting accountability. It never feels good to injure someone; it feels even worse when we do it without justification. We will justify the circumstances out of self-preservation and a wish to save ourselves the agony of owning up to our mistakes.

So, let's apply this to a bigger picture. Therefore, consider how your entire life will alter if accepting responsibility is at the heart of Big Thinking! We illustrated how it functions in relationships by using the example of saying sorry but considering accepting responsibility on a bigger scale.

Let's say that your entire investment was lost in the stock market. The capacity to admit "this was my fault" is astounding, and a small-minded person would do everything possible to avoid dealing with it at all costs. "It was the economy, it was the markets, I was conned, my parents gave me bad advice, etc." is what they will claim. The Big Thinker will have to face up to their accountability for the situation. "I deliberately decided to deposit all of my funds in that account," the Big Thinker would remark while they analyzed the reasons behind the issue. "To make a quick buck, I disregarded sound business standards. I was hurried, naive, and stupid.

What happens next when the Big Thinker takes stock of the situation and admits their guilt? They EXPLORE IT! This is essential! When they transfer the blame to someone else, a tiny thinker forfeits all the lessons they may have learned from an issue like this.

You may be sure you will never succeed in life if you don't allow yourself to fail! You will never realize the dream you may have for yourself if you are unable to accept your shortcomings and failings!

Recall that mastering the Art of Thinking Big entails developing a new life philosophy based on accepting your agency, not merely memorizing a few fast suggestions! When you act out of complete free will and without being forced or coerced, you act with agency. You have the only choice in all you do at the end of the day. In the end, you determine whether you succeed or fail.

Relinquishing control over your life implies that someone else will assume responsibility; even if situations arise, life may present unforeseen obstacles. Individuals in our lives may deceive, injure, or ruin us. But hey, what do you know? Nobody else is going to.

You will undoubtedly deal with individuals who want to give you advice, and there may be people in your life who want to manage things for you, but in the end, you are the only one who has to live with the decisions you make. You can take care of yourself better than any other human could. Big Thinker is aware of this and chooses to own up to it every day, taking full responsibility for both their achievements and mistakes because they understand that no one else can succeed in their place.

So, when things don't go as planned, are you a tiny thinker who throws the blame elsewhere, or are you a big thinker who wants to weigh every setback so that you may learn from it and go forward?

We need to understand that accountability is essential to this change as we concentrate on removing the tiny thoughts preventing us from moving forward. Consider this: the preceding chapter had six noteworthy inadequacies that resulted from limited cognitive capacity. It can't feel good if you nod your head in agreement with any of those six flaws and think, "Yeah, that's me." But now that you've realized it, you may accept accountability for your deeds.

It is unnecessary to hate who you are and harbour feelings of self-loathing to accept responsibility. Nobody is flawless, so there's no benefit in holding yourself to a high ideal of perfection! Saying, "I have been this way; yes, there have been things that have shaped me to act this way, but I am ultimately at fault for all of these choices" means accepting responsibility.

You can alter your behaviours and actions once you acknowledge that you are responsible for them all. You are the only one responsible for them, so you may alter your conduct! By recognizing your bad habits, understanding the reasons behind your actions, and learning how to change them, you may break away from these destructive lifestyle patterns. Saying, "That's just the way I am", is no longer required of you; instead, you are free to state, "I'm growing out of this."

A big thinker is someone who never stops trying to improve himself despite their mistakes and shortfalls. It all begins with taking accountability, owning up to your mistakes, and reflecting on your motivations for your actions. Nothing can dictate your decisions other than you. You are in absolute control, regardless of how you feel.

So, what are some ways you may start taking responsibility for your life? First, you must accept that the procedure isn't pleasant or comfortable. Looking at your bank account with only 4 dollars in it and stating, "This is my fault", isn't nice, no matter how you try to spin it. Realizing that there are no shortcuts to learning to think big and that taking responsibility is frequently painful will help you deal with the discomfort.

Just like a doctor sometimes has to brutally reset a broken limb so that it can recover properly, we must deal with the knowledge that looking our faults in the eye is ultimately for our good. It's the first step to being a Big Thinker and getting to the life you've always wanted. It's not easy, but a Big Thinker isn't someone who is looking for easy. Rather, they are seeking success.

After you've accepted that it might be a hard process to go inward and start taking responsibility for all the things in life that aren't going well without beating yourself up over it, it's time to start thinking in terms of action. It's time to start cultivating vision, the second most critical component to becoming a Big Thinker.

www.ingramcontent.com/pod-product-compliance
Lightning Source LLC
Chambersburg PA
CBHW050203130526
44591CB00034B/1970